POPE FRANCIS: SELECTED PRAYERS

G000256644

Published 2017 by Veritas Publications
7–8 Lower Abbey Street, Dublin 1, Ireland
publications@veritas.ie
www.veritas.ie

ISBN 978 1 84730 796 5

Copyright © Veritas, 2017

10 9 8 7 6 5 4 3 2 1

The material in this publication is protected by copyright law. Except as may be permitted by law, no part of the material may be reproduced (including by storage in a retrieval system) or transmitted in any form or by any means, adapted, rented or lent without the written permission of the copyright owners. Applications for permissions should be addressed to the publisher.

A catalogue record for this book is available from the British Library.

Designed by Lir Mac Cárthaigh, Veritas

Printed in Ireland by KC Print, Killarney, Co Kerry

Veritas books are printed on paper made from the wood pulp of managed forests. For every tree felled, at least one tree is planted, thereby renewing natural resources.

POPE FRANCIS
Selected Prayers

VERITAS

CONTENTS

INTRODUCTION
On Prayer

'When we pray courageously the Lord not only gives us grace; he gives us his very self in the grace. The Lord never gives or sends a grace by post: he brings it himself, he is grace!'

POPE FRANCIS

THE GOSPEL PARABLE* IN LUKE 18: 1-8 CONTAINS an important teaching: we 'ought always to pray and not lose heart' (Lk 18: 1). This means, then, pray constantly, not just when I feel like it. No, Jesus says that we ought 'always to pray and not lose heart'. And he offers the example of the widow and the judge.

The judge is a powerful person, called to issue judgement on the basis of the Law of Moses. That is why the biblical tradition recommended that judges be people who fear God, who are worthy of faith, impartial and incorruptible (cf. Ex 18: 21). However, this judge 'neither feared God nor

---

* The Parable of the Widow and the Unjust Judge

regarded man' (Lk 18: 2). As a judge, he was unfair, unscrupulous, who did not take the Law into account but did whatever he wanted, according to his own interests. It was to him that a widow turned for justice. Widows, along with orphans and foreigners, were the most vulnerable groups of society. The rights afforded them by the Law could be easily disregarded because, being isolated and defenceless, they could hardly be assertive. A poor widow, there, alone, with no one to defend her, might be ignored, might even be denied justice. Just as the orphan, just as the foreigner, the migrant: in that time this was a very serious problem. Faced with the judge's indifference, the widow has recourse to her only weapon: to bother him incessantly with her request for justice. And because of her insistence, she achieves her end. At a certain point, the judge grants her request, not because he is moved by mercy or because his conscience has been working on him; he simply admits: 'because this widow bothers me, I will vindicate her, or she will wear me out by her continual coming' (Lk 18: 5).

From this parable Jesus draws two conclusions: if the widow could manage to bend the dishonest judge with her incessant requests, how much more will God, who is the good and just Father, 'vindicate his elect, who cry to him day and night'; moreover, will not 'delay long over them', but will act 'speedily' (Lk 18: 7-8).

That is why Jesus urges us to pray and 'not to lose heart'. We all go through times of tiredness and discouragement, especially when our prayers seem ineffective. But Jesus assures us: unlike the dishonest judge, God promptly answers his children, even though this doesn't mean he will necessarily do it when and how we would like. Prayer does not work like a magic wand! It helps us keep faith in God, and to entrust ourselves to him even when we do not understand his will. In this, Jesus himself – who prayed constantly! – is our model. The Letter to the Hebrews reminds us that 'In the days of his flesh, Jesus offered up prayers and supplications, with loud cries and tears, to him [God] who was able to save him from death, and he was heard for his godly fear' (Heb 5:7).

At first glance this statement seems far-fetched, because Jesus died on the Cross. Yet, the Letter to the Hebrews makes no mistake: God has indeed saved Jesus from death by giving him complete victory over it, but the path to that [victory] is through death itself! The supplication that God has answered referred to Jesus' prayer in Gethsemane.

Assailed by looming anguish, Jesus prays to the Father to deliver him of this bitter cup of the Passion, but his prayer is pervaded by trust in the Father and he entrusts himself entirely to his will: 'not as I will,' Jesus says, 'but as thou wilt' (Mt 26:39). The object of prayer is of secondary importance; what matters above all is his relationship with the Father. This is what prayer does: it transforms the desire and models it according to the will of God, whatever that may be, because the one who prays aspires first of all to union with God, who is merciful Love.

The parable ends with a question: 'when the Son of man comes, will he find faith on earth?' (Lk 18: 8). And with this question we are all warned: we must not cease to pray, even if left unanswered.

It is prayer that conserves the faith, with out it faith falters! Let us ask the Lord for a faith that is incessant prayer, persevering, like that of the widow in the parable, a faith that nourishes our desire for his coming. And in prayer let us experience that compassion of God, who like a Father comes to encounter his children, full of merciful love.

Pope Francis

From *General Audience,*
St Peter's Square, 25 May 2016

PART ONE
Prayers of Pope Francis

'Prayer, in the face of a problem,
a difficult situation, a calamity, is
opening the door to the Lord so
that he will come.'

POPE FRANCIS

Prayer to Mary, Mother of Silence

Mother of silence, who watches over the mystery
of God,
Save us from the idolatry of the present time, to
which those who forget are condemned.
Purify the eyes of Pastors with the eye-wash of
memory:
Take us back to the freshness of the origins, for a
prayerful, penitent Church.

Mother of the beauty that blossoms from
faithfulness to daily work,
Lift us from the torpor of laziness, pettiness, and
defeatism.
Clothe Pastors in the compassion that unifies,
that makes whole; let us discover the joy of a
humble, brotherly, serving Church.

Mother of tenderness who envelops us in patience and mercy,

Help us burn away the sadness, impatience and rigidity of those who do not know what it means to belong.

Intercede with your Son to obtain that our hands, our feet, our hearts be agile: let us build the Church with the Truth of love.

Mother, we shall be the People of God, pilgrims bound for the Kingdom.

Amen.

Prayer to Mary after the Profession of Faith with the Bishops of the Italian Episcopal Conference, 23 May 2013

Prayer to Mary, Woman of Listening

Mary, woman of listening, open our ears; grant us to know how to listen to the word of your Son Jesus among the thousands of words of this world; grant that we may listen to the reality in which we live, to every person we encounter, especially those who are poor, in need, in hardship.

Mary, woman of decision, illuminate our mind and our heart, so that we may obey, unhesitating, the word of your Son Jesus; give us the courage to decide, not to let ourselves be dragged along, letting others direct our life.

Mary, woman of action, obtain that our hands and feet move 'with haste' toward others, to bring them the charity and love of your Son Jesus, to bring the light of the Gospel to the world, as you did.

Amen.

Prayer to Mary at the conclusion of the recital of the Holy Rosary (Saint Peter's Square, 31 May 2013)

Prayer to the Lord

Lord you left your Mother in our midst that she might accompany us.

May she take care of us and protect us on our journey, in our hearts, in our faith.

May she make us disciples like herself, missionaries like herself.

May she teach us to go out onto the streets.

May she teach us to step outside ourselves.

We bless this image, Lord, which will travel round the country.

May she, by her meekness, by her peace, show us the way.

Lord, you are a scandal. You are a scandal: the scandal of the Cross. A Cross which is humility, meekness; a Cross that speaks to us of God's closeness. We bless this image of the Cross that will travel round the country.

Prayer at the conclusion of the meeting with the young people from Argentina gathered in the Cathedral of São Sebastião (25 July 2013)

Prayer to the Lord (II)

Lord God look down upon us! Look at this city, this island. Look upon our families.

Lord, you were not without a job, you were a carpenter, you were happy.

Lord, we have no work.

The idols want to rob us of our dignity. The unjust systems want to rob us of hope.

Lord, do not leave us on our own. Help us to help each other; so that we forget our selfishness a little and feel in our heart the 'we', the we of a people who want to keep on going.

Lord Jesus, you were never out of work, give us work and teach us to fight for work and bless us all. In the name of the Father, of the Son and of the Holy Spirit. Amen.

Prayer to the Lord at the conclusion of the meeting with workers (Cagliari, 22 September 2013)

Act of Entrustment to the Blessed Virgin Mary of Fatima

Blessed Virgin Mary of Fatima,
with renewed gratitude for your motherly presence
we join in the voice of all generations that call you
   blessed.

We celebrate in you the great works of God,
who never tires of lowering himself in mercy over
   humanity,
afflicted by evil and wounded by sin,
to heal and to save it.

Accept with the benevolence of a Mother
this act of entrustment that we make in faith
    today,
before this your image, beloved to us.
We are certain that each one of us is precious in
    your eyes
and that nothing in our hearts has estranged you.

May that we allow your sweet gaze
to reach us and the perpetual warmth of your
    smile.

Guard our life with your embrace:
bless and strengthen every desire for good;
give new life and nourishment to faith;
sustain and enlighten hope;
awaken and animate charity;
guide us all on the path to holiness.

Teach us your own special love for the little and
    the poor,
for the excluded and the suffering,
for sinners and the wounded of heart:

gather all people under you protection
and give us all to your beloved Son, our Lord
Jesus.

Amen.

---

*Act of entrustment to Mary, Virgin of Fatima, at
the conclusion of Mass on the occasion of the Marian
Day (Saint Peter's Square, 13 October 2013)*

Prayer to Mary Immaculate

Virgin most holy and immaculate,
to you, the honour of our people,
and the loving protector of our city,
do we turn with loving trust.

You are all-beautiful, O Mary!
In you there is no sin.

Awaken in all of us a renewed desire for holiness:
May the splendour of truth shine forth in our words,
the song of charity resound in our works,
purity and chastity abide in our hearts and bodies,
and the full beauty of the Gospel be evident in
   our lives.

You are all-beautiful, O Mary!
In you the Word of God became flesh.

Help us always to heed the Lord's voice:
May we never be indifferent to the cry of the
    poor,
or untouched by the sufferings of the sick and
    those in need;
may we be sensitive to the loneliness of the elderly
    and the vulnerability of children,
and always love and cherish the life of every
    human being.

You are all-beautiful, O Mary!
In you is the fullness of joy born of life with God.

Help us never to forget the meaning of our
    earthly journey:
May the kindly light of faith illumine our days,
the comforting power of hope direct our steps,
the contagious warmth of love stir our hearts;
and may our gaze be fixed on God, in whom true
    joy is found.

You are all-beautiful, O Mary!
Hear our prayer, graciously hear our plea:

May the beauty of God's merciful love in Jesus
    abide in our hearts,
and may this divine beauty save us, our city and
    the entire world.

Amen.

Act of veneration to the Blessed Virgin Mary at the
Spanish Steps on the occasion of the Solemnity of the
Immaculate Conception (8 December 2013)

Act of Consecration to Our Lady of Aparecida

Mary Most Holy by the merits of Our Lord Jesus Christ, in your beloved image of Aparecida, spread infinite favours over all Brazil.

I, unworthy to be counted among your sons and daughters but full of desire to share in the blessings of your mercy, lie prostrate at your feet. To you I consecrate my intentions, that they may ever dwell on the love that you merit; to you I consecrate my tongue that it may ever praise you and spread your devotion; to you I consecrate my heart, that, after God, I may love you above all things.

Receive me, incomparable Queen, you whom Christ Crucified gave to us as Mother, and count me among your blessed sons and daughters; take me under your protection; come to my aid in all my needs, both spiritual and temporal, and above all at the hour of my death.

Bless me, heavenly helper, and through your powerful intercession, give me strength in my weakness, so that, by serving you faithfully in this life, I may praise you, love you and give you thanks in heaven, for all eternity. Let it be!

Act of Consecration to Our Lady of Aparecida during Mass in the Basilica of the Shrine of Our Lady of the Conception of Aparecida (24 July 2013)

Prayer for Peace

Lord God of peace, hear our prayer!

We have tried so many times and over so many
years to resolve our conflicts by our own powers
and by the force of our arms. How many moments
of hostility and darkness have we experienced;
how much blood has been shed; how many lives
have been shattered; how many hopes have been
buried ... But our efforts have been in vain.

Now, Lord, come to our aid! Grant us peace,
teach us peace; guide our steps in the way of
peace. Open our eyes and our hearts, and give us
the courage to say: 'Never again war!'; 'With war
everything is lost'. Instil in our hearts the courage
to take concrete steps to achieve peace.

Lord, God of Abraham, God of the Prophets,
God of Love, you created us and you call us to

live as brothers and sisters. Give us the strength daily to be instruments of peace; enable us to see everyone who crosses our path as our brother or sister. Make us sensitive to the plea of our citizens who entreat us to turn our weapons of war into implements of peace, our trepidation into confident trust, and our quarreling into forgiveness.

Keep alive within us the flame of hope, so that with patience and perseverance we may opt for dialogue and reconciliation. In this way may peace triumph at last, and may the words 'division', 'hatred' and 'war' be banished from the heart of every man and woman. Lord, defuse the violence of our tongues and our hands. Renew our hearts and minds, so that the word which always brings us together will be 'brother', and our way of life will always be that of: Shalom, Peace, Salaam!

Amen.

Invocation for peace (8 June 2014)

Prayer on the Feast of the Immaculate Conception

Mary our Mother,

Today the People of God celebrate, they venerate you, the Immaculate, ever preserved from the stain of sin.

Accept the homage I offer you in the name of the Church in Rome and throughout the world.

Knowing that you, our Mother, are totally free from sin is a consolation to us.

Knowing that evil has no power over you fills us with hope and strength in our daily struggle against the threat of the evil one.

But in this struggle we are not alone, we are not orphans, for Jesus, before dying on the Cross, gave you to us as our Mother.

Though we are sinners, we are still your children, the children of the Immaculate, called to that holiness that has shown resplendent in you by the grace of God from the beginning.

Inspired by this hope, today we invoke your motherly protection for us, our families, this city and the world.

Through your intercession, may the power of God's love that preserved you from original sin, free humanity from every form of spiritual and material slavery and make God's plan of salvation victorious in hearts and in history.

May grace prevail over pride in us, too, your children.
May we become merciful as our heavenly Father is merciful.

In this time leading up to the celebration of Jesus' birth, teach us to go against the current: to strip ourselves, to be humble, and giving, to listen and be silent, to go out of ourselves, granting space to the beauty of God, the source of true joy.

Pray for us, our Immaculate Mother!

Act of Veneration to the Immaculate Conception at the Spanish Steps (8 December 2014)

Prayer to the 'Virgen De La Caridad'

Our Lady of Charity of El Cobre,
Patroness of Cuba!
Hail, Mary,
full of grace!
You are the beloved Daughter of the Father,
Mother of Christ, our God,
the living Temple
of the Holy Spirit.

You carry in your name,
Virgin of Charity,
the memory of God who is Love,
the memory of the new commandments of Jesus,
the evocation of the Holy Spirit:
love poured into our hearts,

the fire of charity
sent on Pentecost
upon the Church,
the gift of the full freedom
of the children of God.

Blessed are you among women
and blessed is the fruit
of your womb, Jesus!
You came to visit our people
And you chose to remain with us
As Mother and Lady of Cuba,
on our pilgrimage
through the paths of history.

Your name and your image
are carved
into the hearts and minds
of all Cubans,
both in the Country and abroad,
as a sign of hope
and the centre of brotherly communion.

Holy Mary, Mother of God
and our Mother!

Pray for us
before your Son Jesus Christ,
intercede for us
with your motherly heart,
flooded with the love of the Holy Spirit.
Increase our faith,
awaken our hope,
broaden and strengthen our love.

Watch over our families,
protect our young people and our children,
console those who suffer.
Be the mother of the faithful
and of the pastors of the Church,
model and star of the new evangelisation.
Mother of reconciliation!
Gather your people
scattered around the earth.
Make of our Cuban nation
a house of brothers and sisters

that this people may open wide
her mind, her heart
and her life to Christ,
the one Saviour and Redeemer,
who lives and reigns with the Father
and the Holy Spirit
forever and ever.

Amen.

---

*Shrine of the 'Virgen de la Caridad del Cobre',
Santiago de Cuba (Monday, 21 September 2015)*

Prayer of Remembrance for the Victims of 9/11

O God of love, compassion, and healing,
look on us, people of many different faiths
and religious traditions,
who gather today on this hallowed ground,
the scene of unspeakable violence and pain.

We ask you in your goodness
to give eternal light and peace
to all who died here:
the heroic first-responders:
our fire fighters, police officers,
emergency service workers
and Port Authority personnel,
along with all the innocent men and women
who were victims of this tragedy

simply because their work or service
brought them here on September 11.

We ask you, in your compassion,
to bring healing to those who,
because of their presence here fourteen years ago,
continue to suffer from injuries and illness.

Heal, too, the pain of still-grieving families
and all who lost loved ones in this tragedy.
Give them strength to continue their lives
with courage and hope.

We are mindful as well
of those who suffered death, injury, and loss
on the same day at the Pentagon
and in Shanksville, Pennsylvania.
Our hearts are one with theirs
as our prayer embraces their pain and suffering.

God of peace, bring your peace to our violent world:
peace in the hearts of all men and women
and peace among the nations of the earth.

Turn to your way of love
those whose hearts and minds
are consumed with hatred,
and who justify killing in the name of religion.

God of understanding,
overwhelmed by the magnitude of this tragedy,
we seek your light and guidance
as we confront such terrible events.

Grant that those whose lives were spared
may live so that the lives lost here
may not have been lost in vain.

Comfort and console us, strengthen us in hope,
and give us the wisdom and courage
to work tirelessly for a world
where true peace and love reign
among nations and in the hearts of all.

*Interreligious Meeting at the Ground Zero
Memorial in New York, 25 December 2015, during
Apostolic Journey to the United States*

Prayer for the Extraordinary Jubilee of Mercy

Lord Jesus Christ,
you have taught us to be merciful like the
heavenly Father,
and have told us that whoever sees you sees Him.
Show us your face and we will be saved.
Your loving gaze freed Zacchaeus and Matthew
from being enslaved by money;
the adulteress and Magdalene from seeking
happiness only in created things;
made Peter weep after his betrayal,
and assured Paradise to the repentant thief.
Let us hear, as if addressed to each one of us,
the words that you spoke to the Samaritan
woman:
'If you knew the gift of God!'

You are the visible face of the invisible Father,
of the God who manifests his power above all by
forgiveness and mercy:
let the Church be your visible face in the world,
its Lord risen and glorified.
You willed that your ministers would also be
clothed in weakness
in order that they may feel compassion for those
in ignorance and error:
let everyone who approaches them feel sought
after, loved, and forgiven by God.

Send your Spirit and consecrate every one of us
with its anointing,
so that the Jubilee of Mercy may be a year of grace
from the Lord,
and your Church, with renewed enthusiasm, may
bring good news to the poor,
proclaim liberty to captives and the oppressed,
and restore sight to the blind.

We ask this of you, Lord Jesus, through the
  intercession of Mary, Mother of
Mercy; you who live and reign with the Father
  and the Holy Spirit for ever and ever.

Amen.

---

*The Jubilee of Mercy was a special year-long period
of prayer held from 8 December 2015 to
20 November 2016*

Prayer on the Feast of the Immaculate Conception (II)

O Mary, our Immaculate Mother,
On your feast day I come to you,
And I come not alone:
I bring with me all those with whom your Son
    entrusted to me,
In this city of Rome and in the entire world,
That you may bless them and preserve them from
    harm.

I bring to you, Mother, children,
Especially those who are alone, abandoned,
And for this reason are tricked and exploited.
I bring to you, Mother, families,
Who carry forward life and society

With their daily and hidden efforts;
In a special way the families who struggle the
    most
For their many internal and external problems.
I bring to you, Mother, all workers, both men and
    women,
And I entrust to you especially those who, out of
    need,
Are forced to work in an unworthy profession
And those who have lost work or are unable to
    find it.

We are in need of your immaculate gaze,
To rediscover the ability to look upon persons and
    things
With respect and awareness,
Without egotistical or hypocritical interests.
We are in need of your immaculate heart,
To love freely,
Without secondary aims but seeking the good of
    the other,
With simplicity and sincerity, renouncing masks
    and tricks.

We are in need of your immaculate hands,
To caress with tenderness,
To touch the flesh of Jesus
In our poor, sick, or despised brethren,
To raise up those who have fallen and support
those who waver.
We are in need of your immaculate feet,
To go toward those who know not how to make
the first step,
To walk on the paths of those who are lost,
To find those who feel alone.

We thank you, O Mother, because in showing
yourself to us
You free us of all stain of sin;
You remind us that what comes first is the grace
of God,
The love of Jesus Christ who gave his life for us,
The strength of the Holy Spirit which renews all
things.
Let us not give in to discouragement,
But, trusting in your constant help,
Let us engage ourselves fully in renewal of self,

Of this city and of the entire world.
Pray for us, Holy Mother of God!

*Solemnity of the Immaculate Conception at the
Spanish Steps in Rome (8 December 2016)*

❦

PART TWO
Prayers from Francis'
Papal Documents

'The Lord tells us: "the first task
in life is this – prayer". But not the
prayer of words, like a parrot; but
the prayer, the heart: gazing on the
Lord.'

PODE FRANCIS

Prayer to the Blessed Virgin Mary

Mary, Virgin and Mother,
you who, moved by the Holy Spirit,
welcomed the word of life
in the depths of your humble faith:
as you gave yourself completely to the Eternal One,
help us to say our own 'yes'
to the urgent call, as pressing as ever,
to proclaim the good news of Jesus.
Filled with Christ's presence,
you brought joy to John the Baptist,
making him exult in the womb of his mother.
Brimming over with joy,
you sang of the great things done by God.
Standing at the foot of the cross
with unyielding faith,
you received the joyful comfort of the
    Resurrection,

and joined the disciples in awaiting the Spirit
so that the evangelising Church might be born.
Obtain for us now a new ardour born of the
    Resurrection,
that we may bring to all the Gospel of life
which triumphs over death.
Give us a holy courage to seek new paths,
that the gift of unfading beauty
may reach every man and woman.

Virgin of listening and contemplation,
Mother of love, Bride of the eternal wedding
    feast,
pray for the Church, whose pure icon you are,
that she may never be closed in on herself
or lose her passion for establishing God's
    kingdom.

Star of the new evangelisation,
help us to bear radiant witness to communion,
service, ardent and generous faith,
justice and love of the poor,
that the joy of the Gospel

may reach to the ends of the earth,
illuminating even the fringes of our world.
Mother of the living Gospel,
wellspring of happiness for God's little ones,
pray for us.

Amen.
Alleluia!

From Evangelii Gaudium: The Joy of the
Gospel, *the Apostolic Exhortation on the
Proclamation of the Gospel in Today's World
(24 November 2013)*

Prayer to the Holy Family

Jesus, Mary and Joseph,
in you we contemplate
the splendour of true love;
to you we turn with trust.

Holy Family of Nazareth,
grant that our families too
may be places of communion and prayer,
authentic schools of the Gospel
and small domestic churches.

Holy Family of Nazareth,
may families never again experience
violence, rejection and division;
may all who have been hurt or scandalised
find ready comfort and healing.

Holy Family of Nazareth,
make us once more mindful
of the sacredness and inviolability of the family,
and its beauty in God's plan.

Jesus, Mary and Joseph,
Graciously hear our prayer.

Amen.

From Amoris Laetitia: The Joy of Love,
Apostolic Exhortation on Love in the Family
(19 March 2016)

Prayer to the Mother of our Church and of our Faith

Mother, help our faith!

Open our ears to hear God's word and to recognise his voice and call.

Awaken in us a desire to follow in his footsteps, to go forth from our own land and to receive his promise.

Help us to be touched by his love, that we may touch him in faith.

Help us to entrust ourselves fully to him and to believe in his love, especially at times of trial, beneath the shadow of the cross, when our faith is called to mature.

Sow in our faith the joy of the Risen One.

Remind us that those who believe are never alone.

Teach us to see all things with the eyes of Jesus, that he may be light for our path. And may this light of faith always increase in us, until the dawn of that undying day which is Christ himself, your Son, our Lord!

From Lumen Fidei, *Encyclical Letter, to the Bishops, Priests, and Deacons, Consecrated Persons and the Lay Faithful on Faith (29 June 2013)*

A Prayer for our Earth

All-powerful God, you are present in the whole
    universe
and in the smallest of your creatures.
You embrace with your tenderness all that exists.
Pour out upon us the power of your love,
that we may protect life and beauty.
Fill us with peace, that we may live
as brothers and sisters, harming no one.
O God of the poor,
help us to rescue the abandoned and forgotten of
    this earth,
so precious in your eyes.
Bring healing to our lives,
that we may protect the world and not prey on it,
that we may sow beauty, not pollution and
    destruction.

Touch the hearts
of those who look only for gain
at the expense of the poor and the earth.
Teach us to discover the worth of each thing,
to be filled with awe and contemplation,
to recognise that we are profoundly united
with every creature
as we journey towards your infinite light.
We thank you for being with us each day.
Encourage us, we pray, in our struggle
for justice, love and peace.

From Laudato Si': Praised Be, *Encyclical Letter
on Care for Our Common Home (24 May 2015)*

A Christian Prayer in Union with Creation

Father, we praise you with all your creatures.
They came forth from your all-powerful hand;
they are yours, filled with your presence and your
    tender love.
Praise be to you!

Son of God, Jesus,
through you all things were made.
You were formed in the womb of Mary our
    Mother,
you became part of this earth,
and you gazed upon this world with human eyes.
Today you are alive in every creature
in your risen glory.
Praise be to you!

Holy Spirit, by your light
you guide this world towards the Father's love
and accompany creation as it groans in travail.
You also dwell in our hearts
and you inspire us to do what is good.
Praise be to you!

Triune Lord, wondrous community of infinite love,
teach us to contemplate you
in the beauty of the universe,
for all things speak of you.
Awaken our praise and thankfulness
for every being that you have made.
Give us the grace to feel profoundly joined
to everything that is.

God of love, show us our place in this world
as channels of your love
for all the creatures of this earth,
for not one of them is forgotten in your sight.

Enlighten those who possess power and money
that they may avoid the sin of indifference,

that they may love the common good, advance the
    weak,
and care for this world in which we live.
The poor and the earth are crying out.
O Lord, seize us with your power and light,
help us to protect all life,
to prepare for a better future,
for the coming of your Kingdom
of justice, peace, love and beauty.
Praise be to you!
Amen.

From Laudato Si': Praised Be, *Encyclical Letter
on Care for Our Common Home (24 May 2015)*

PART THREE
Prayers Beloved of Pope Francis

'May the Lord help us to
understand [the] link between
prayer and hope. Prayer leads you
forward in hope, and when things
become dark, more prayer is needed!
And there will be more hope.'

POPE FRANCIS

A Prayer Before the Crucifix

BY ST FRANCIS OF ASSISI

Having taken the name Francis as pontiff it's little wonder that the pope has a particular devotion to his namesake, St Francis of Assisi. During the Exposition of the Holy Shroud on Holy Saturday 2013, Francis quoted the following prayer.

Most High, glorious God,
enlighten the shadows of my heart,
and grant me a right faith, a certain hope and
    perfect charity,
sense and understanding, Lord,
so that I may accomplish your holy and true
    command.

Amen.

Prayer for Good Humour

BY ST THOMAS MORE

During a Christmas address to the Roman Curia on 22 December 2014, Pope Francis said: 'A bit of good humour is very good for us! It will do us much good to pray St Thomas More's prayer frequently: I pray it every day, and it helps me'.

Grant me, O Lord, good digestion, and also
     something to digest.
Grant me a healthy body, and the necessary good
     humor to maintain it.
Grant me a simple soul that knows to treasure all
     that is good
and that doesn't frighten easily at the sight of evil,
but rather finds the means to put things back in
     their place.

Give me a soul that knows not boredom,
      grumblings, sighs and laments,
nor excess of stress, because of that obstructing
      thing called 'I'.
Grant me, O Lord, a sense of good humour.
Allow me the grace to be able to take a joke to
      discover in life a bit of joy,
and to be able to share it with others.

Prayer to Our Lady, Untier of Knots

When Pope Francis was studying in Germany in the mid-1980s he came across a Baroque painting by Johann Georg Melchior Schmidtner which depicted Our Lady – suspended between heaven and earth – serenely untying a knotted white ribbon. Since then, Francis has had a special devotion to 'Our Lady, Untier of Knots' which he shared with the people of Argentina as Archbishop of Buenos Aires. The prayer below is often used to introduce a special novena to Our Lady, Untier of Knots.

Holy Mary, full of God's presence during the days of your life, you accepted with full humility the Father's will, and the Devil was never capable of tying you around with his confusion.

Once with your son you interceded for our difficulties, and, full of kindness and patience, you gave us example of how to untie the knots of our life.

And by remaining forever Our Mother, you put in order and make clearer the ties that link us to the Lord.

Holy Mother, Mother of God, and our Mother, to you, who untie with motherly heart the knots of our life, we pray to you to receive in your hands [name of person], and to free him/her of the knots and confusion with which our enemy attacks. Through your grace, your intercession, and your example, deliver us from all evil, Our Lady, and untie the knots that prevent us from being united with God, so that we, free from sin and error, may find Him in all things, may have our hearts placed in Him, and may serve Him always in our brothers and sisters.

Amen.

Five Finger Prayer

This method of prayer, championed by Pope Francis, has been widely adopted in classrooms and parishes across the globe, and has resonated particularly with children and young people.

1. **The Thumb**
   The closest finger to you reminds you to pray for those who are closest to us, like our family and friends.

2. **The Index Finger**
   The pointing finger reminds you to pray for wisdom and support for those who teach us and show us the way.

3. **The Middle Finger**
   The tallest finger reminds you to pray for guidance for our leaders and those in positions of authority.

4. **The Ring Finger**

   Our weakest finger reminds you to pray for
   the weakest in society, like those who are sick,
   poor or are having problems.

5. **The Little Finger**

   The smallest finger reminds you to pray for
   yourself. When you have prayed for the other
   four groups, you will be able to see your own
   needs, but from the proper perspective.

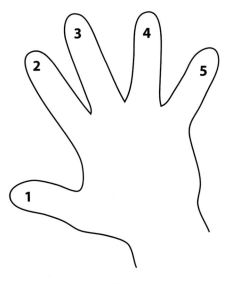